The

HOLY BIBLE

LEGACY STANDARD BIBLE

——— ∽ ———

Containing the Gospel According to

JOHN

LEGACY STANDARD BIBLE
Gospel of John
Copyright © 2021 by The LOCKMAN Foundation
A Corporation Not for Profit, La Habra, California, All Rights Reserved Lockman.org
The Legacy Standard Bible is adapted from the New American Standard Bible
Copyright © 1960, 1971, 1977, 1995 by The Lockman Foundation, All Rights Reserved
The "LSB" and "Legacy Standard Bible" are trademarks of The Lockman Foundation,
All rights reserved. Managed in partnership with Three Sixteen Publishing Inc.
For inquiries regarding licensing and trademarks, or to quote the LSB, please visit LSBible.org
Learn about our mission of distributing free Bibles. LegacyBibleFoundation.com.
Printed in China by codra.com ◊ 29 28 27 26 25 / 2 3 4 5 6. ALL RIGHTS RESERVED.

STEADFAST BIBLES is a division of THREE SIXTEEN PUBLISHING
Southern California

978-1-63664-380-9

God's Plan of Salvation

YOUR PROBLEM

Everyone is destined to die, but life does not end with death. The Bible says that after death there will be a judgment where each person will give an account of his or her life before God (Hebrews 4:13; 9:27). When we die, we will either live with God forever in Heaven or be separated from God in Hell.

Unfortunately, humanity's sinful nature and our ongoing choices to sin result in our living in disobedience to God: "for all have sinned and fall short of the glory of God" (Romans 3:23). This is humanity's problem: because of sin, every person is separated from God (Isaiah 59:2) and destined to spend eternity separated from Him.

People have tried to overcome this separation in many ways: by doing good, by practicing religion, by creating their own ideas of salvation, or by attempting to live a good moral life. However, none of these things is enough to cross the barrier of separation between God and humanity, because God is holy and human beings are sinful (Isaiah 64:6). Regardless of how good you think you are, every human has lied, stolen, hated, or otherwise disobeyed God's perfect will. We need to be saved from our sins and the judgment of God.

GOD'S LOVE

Yet, there is hope. Listen to the words of Jesus found in the very book you are holding in your hands:

> For God so loved the world, that He gave His only begotten Son, that whoever believes in Him shall not perish, but have eternal life. (John 3:16)

Although God has every right to condemn every person, because of His love He sent His Son, Jesus Christ. Jesus, the Son of God, was born as a man, lived a perfectly sinless life, and then was crucified. Since God is not a corrupt Judge, He does not simply sweep our sins under the rug—someone needs to be punished for them. Jesus sacrificed Himself to die on the cross to take the punishment of God that we deserve.

After Jesus Christ died on the cross, the Bible says that He rose from the dead! His resurrection life is a guarantee that Christians will also have eternal life. Eternal life not just about living forever, it's about having a loving relationship with God:

> And this is eternal life, that they may know You, the only true God, and Jesus Christ whom You have sent. (John 17:3)

WHAT NOW?

If you acknowledge that you are separated from God because you are a sinner who is in need of salvation, Scripture says you can receive God's gracious gift of eternal life—not by working for it—but by simply trusting in Jesus for salvation. Turn from your sins, and put your faith in Jesus as your Lord and Savior.

Begin attending a Christian church that preaches and teaches the Bible, share your newfound faith with others, and prayerfully read through the book you hold in your hands. The Apostle John lets us know why he wrote this book:

> but these have been written so that you may believe that Jesus is the Christ, the Son of God; and that believing you may have life in His name. (John 20:31)

May this narrative of the life of Jesus, as told by one of His closest friends, lead you to trust and believe in Him.

EXPLANATION OF TERMINOLOGY

The Bible is actually a collection of 66 books, originally written in Hebrew, Aramaic, and Greek. Since the Legacy Standard Bible (LSB) translation is committed to precisely representing what was written in the original languages, certain Greek terms used throughout the Gospel of John may differ slightly from how some modern English speakers understand those same terms.

The Terminology of Slave: The Greek term doulos, translated in the LSB as "slave", refers to an economic situation where someone was owned by another person. Unlike the transatlantic slave trade, ancient slavery was primarily a financial institution, was often entered into voluntarily (e.g., to pay off debt or to escape poverty), and was not normally motivated by racism. The Bible does not shy away from this term because it condemns all wicked forms of slavery (i.e., to sin, Satan, and death), highlights the power of redemption, and affirms that Christians were slaves of sin, but now are slaves belonging to the Lord Jesus Christ (Romans 6:16–22).

Gender Language: The LSB seeks to literally translate what was written in John's original Greek. The Greek language often used masculine words to describe both men and women, depending on the context. The word "man" can refer generically to "humanity", "he" can refer generically to a person "he/she", and so on.

Learn more about the Legacy Standard Bible translation
at LSBible.org

EXPLANATION OF GENERAL FORMAT

Personal pronouns are capitalized when pertaining to Deity.

Italics are used in the text to indicate words which are not found in the original Greek but implied by it.

Small caps in the NT are used in the text to indicate OT quotations or obvious references to OT texts.

Asterisks are used to mark present tense verbs in Greek which have been translated with an English past tense in order to conform to modern usage (i.e., historical presents). The translators recognized that in some contexts the present tense seems more unexpected and unjustified to the English reader than a past tense would have been. For the sake of heightened vividness, Greek authors frequently used the present tense thereby transporting their readers in imagination to the actual scene at the time of occurrence. However, the translators felt that it would be wise to change these historical presents to English past tenses.

Brackets in text indicate words probably not in the original writings.

See "Foreword to the LSB" at LSBible.org
for more explanation of specific formatting styles.

The Gospel According to

JOHN

The Deity of Jesus Christ

1 In the beginning was the Word, and the Word was with God, and the Word was God. ²He was in the beginning with God. ³All things came into being through Him, and apart from Him nothing came into being that has come into being. ⁴In Him was life, and the life was the Light of men. ⁵And the Light shines in the darkness, and the darkness did not overtake it.

The Witness of John the Baptist

⁶There was a man having been sent from God, whose name was John. ⁷He came as a witness, to bear witness about the Light, so that all might believe through him. ⁸He was not the Light, but *he came* to bear witness about the Light.

JOHN 1:9

⁹ There was the true Light which, coming into the world, enlightens everyone. ¹⁰ He was in the world, and the world was made through Him, and the world did not know Him. ¹¹ He came to what was His own, and those who were His own did not receive Him. ¹² But as many as received Him, to them He gave the right to become children of God, *even* to those who believe in His name, ¹³ who were born, not of blood nor of the will of the flesh nor of the will of man, but of God.

The Word Became Flesh

¹⁴ And the Word became flesh, and dwelt among us, and we beheld His glory, glory as of the only begotten from the Father, full of grace and truth. ¹⁵ John *bore witness about Him and cried out, saying, "This was He of whom I said, 'He who comes after me has been ahead of me, for He existed before me.'" ¹⁶ For of His fullness we have all received, and grace upon grace. ¹⁷ For the Law was given through Moses; grace and truth came through Jesus Christ. ¹⁸ No one has seen God at any time; the only begotten God who is in the bosom of the Father, He has explained *Him*.

A Voice in the Wilderness

¹⁹ And this is the witness of John, when the Jews sent to him priests and Levites from Jerusalem to ask him, "Who are you?" ²⁰ And he confessed and did not deny, but confessed, "I am not the Christ." ²¹ And they asked him, "What then? Are you Elijah?" And he *said, "I am not." "Are you the Prophet?" And he answered, "No." ²² Therefore, they said to him, "Who are you, so that we may give an answer to those who sent us? What do you say about yourself?" ²³ He said, "I am A VOICE OF ONE CRYING IN THE WILDERNESS, 'MAKE STRAIGHT THE WAY OF THE LORD,' as Isaiah the prophet said."

²⁴ Now they had been sent from the Pharisees. ²⁵ And they asked him, and said to him, "Why then are you baptizing, if you are not the Christ, nor Elijah, nor the Prophet?" ²⁶ John answered them, saying, "I baptize with water, *but* among you stands One whom you do not know. ²⁷ *This One is* He who comes after me, of whom I am not worthy to untie the strap of His sandal." ²⁸ These things took place in Bethany beyond the Jordan, where John was baptizing.

²⁹ On the next day, he *saw Jesus coming to him

and *said, "Behold, the Lamb of God who takes away the sin of the world! ³⁰ This is He of whom I said, 'After me comes a man who has been ahead of me, for He existed before me.' ³¹ I did not know Him, but so that He might be manifested to Israel, I came baptizing with water." ³² And John bore witness saying, "I have beheld the Spirit descending as a dove out of heaven, and He abided on Him. ³³ And I did not know Him, but He who sent me to baptize with water said to me, 'The One upon whom you see the Spirit descending and abiding on Him, this is the One who baptizes with the Holy Spirit.' ³⁴ And I myself have seen, and have borne witness that this is the Son of God."

Behold, the Lamb of God

³⁵ On the next day, John again was standing with two of his disciples, ³⁶ and he looked at Jesus as He walked, and *said, "Behold, the Lamb of God!" ³⁷ And the two disciples heard him speak and followed Jesus. ³⁸ And when Jesus turned and noticed them following, He *said to them, "What do you seek?" They said to Him, "Rabbi (which translated means Teacher), where are You staying?"

[39] He *said to them, "Come, and you will see." So they came and saw where He was staying; and they stayed with Him that day. It was about the tenth hour. [40] One of the two who heard John *speak* and followed Him, was Andrew, Simon Peter's brother. [41] He first *found his own brother Simon and *said to him, "We have found the Messiah" (which translated means Christ). [42] He brought him to Jesus. When Jesus looked at him, He said, "You are Simon the son of John; you shall be called Cephas" (which is translated Peter).

[43] On the next day, He desired to go into Galilee, and He *found Philip. And Jesus *said to him, "Follow Me." [44] Now Philip was from Bethsaida, the city of Andrew and Peter. [45] Philip *found Nathanael and *said to him, "We have found Him of whom Moses in the Law and *also* the Prophets wrote—Jesus of Nazareth, the son of Joseph." [46] And Nathanael said to him, "Can any good thing come out of Nazareth?" Philip *said to him, "Come and see." [47] Jesus saw Nathanael coming to Him, and *said about him, "Behold, truly an Israelite in whom there is no deceit!" [48] Nathanael *said to Him, "From where do You know me?"

Jesus answered and said to him, "Before Philip called you, when you were under the fig tree, I saw you." ⁴⁹ Nathanael answered Him, "Rabbi, You are the Son of God; You are the King of Israel." ⁵⁰ Jesus answered and said to him, "Because I said to you that I saw you under the fig tree, do you believe? You will see greater things than these." ⁵¹ And He *said to him, "Truly, truly, I say to you, you will see THE HEAVENS OPENED AND THE ANGELS OF GOD ASCENDING AND DESCENDING on the Son of Man."

The Wedding at Cana

2 And on the third day there was a wedding in Cana of Galilee, and the mother of Jesus was there; ² and both Jesus and His disciples were invited to the wedding. ³ And when the wine ran out, the mother of Jesus *said to Him, "They have no wine." ⁴ And Jesus *said to her, "Woman, what do I have to do with you? My hour has not yet come." ⁵ His mother *said to the servants, "Whatever He says to you, do *it*." ⁶ Now there were six stone water jars set there for the Jewish custom of purification, containing ᵃtwo or three measures

---

a. Approx. 20-30 gal. or 75-115 l, a measure was approx. 10 gal. or 38 l each. ⁷Jesus *said to them, "Fill the water jars with water." So they filled them up to the brim. ⁸And He *said to them, "Draw *some* out now and take it to the headwaiter." So they took it *to him.* ⁹Now when the headwaiter tasted the water which had become wine, and did not know where it came from (but the servants who had drawn the water knew), the headwaiter *called the bridegroom, ¹⁰and *said to him, "Every man serves the good wine first, and when *the people* have drunk freely, *then* the inferior *wine*; *but* you have kept the good wine until now." ¹¹Jesus did this in Cana of Galilee as the beginning of *His* signs, and manifested His glory, and His disciples believed in Him.

¹²After this He went down to Capernaum, He and His mother and *His* brothers and His disciples; and they stayed there a few days.

Jesus Cleanses the Temple

¹³And the Passover of the Jews was near, and Jesus went up to Jerusalem. ¹⁴And He found in the temple those who were selling oxen and sheep and doves, and the money changers seated *at their tables.* ¹⁵And He made a scourge of cords,

and drove *them* all out of the temple, with the sheep and the oxen; and He poured out the coins of the money changers and overturned their tables; ¹⁶ and to those who were selling the doves He said, "Take these things away; stop making My Father's house a place of business." ¹⁷ His disciples remembered that it was written, "ZEAL FOR YOUR HOUSE WILL CONSUME ME." ¹⁸ The Jews then said to Him, "What sign do You show us as your authority for doing these things?" ¹⁹ Jesus answered them, "Destroy this sanctuary, and in three days I will raise it up." ²⁰ The Jews then said, "It took forty-six years to build this sanctuary, and will You raise it up in three days?" ²¹ But He was speaking about the sanctuary of His body. ²² So when He was raised from the dead, His disciples remembered that He said this; and they believed the Scripture and the word which Jesus had spoken.

²³ Now when He was in Jerusalem at the Passover, during the feast, many believed in His name, when they saw His signs which He was doing. ²⁴ But Jesus, on His part, was not entrusting Himself to them, for He knew all men, ²⁵ and because He had no need that anyone bear witness

concerning man, for He Himself knew what was in man.

You Must Be Born Again

3 Now there was a man of the Pharisees, named Nicodemus, a ruler of the Jews; ²this man came to Jesus by night and said to Him, "Rabbi, we know that You have come from God *as* a teacher; for no one can do these signs that You do unless God is with him." ³Jesus answered and said to him, "Truly, truly, I say to you, unless one is born again he cannot see the kingdom of God."

⁴Nicodemus *said to Him, "How can a man be born when he is old? Can he enter a second time into his mother's womb and be born?" ⁵Jesus answered, "Truly, truly, I say to you, unless one is born of water and the Spirit he cannot enter into the kingdom of God. ⁶That which has been born of the flesh is flesh, and that which has been born of the Spirit is spirit. ⁷Do not marvel that I said to you, 'You must be born again.' ⁸The wind blows where it wishes and you hear its sound, but do not know where it comes from and where it is going; so is everyone who has been born of the Spirit."

JOHN 3:9

⁹ Nicodemus answered and said to Him, "How can these things be?" ¹⁰ Jesus answered and said to him, "Are you the teacher of Israel and do not understand these things? ¹¹ Truly, truly, I say to you, we speak of what we know and bear witness of what we have seen, and you do not accept our witness. ¹² If I told you earthly things and you do not believe, how will you believe if I tell you heavenly things? ¹³ And no one has ascended into heaven, but He who descended from heaven, the Son of Man. ¹⁴ And as Moses lifted up the serpent in the wilderness, even so must the Son of Man be lifted up; ¹⁵ so that whoever believes will in Him have eternal life.

¹⁶ "For God so loved the world, that He gave His only begotten Son, that whoever believes in Him shall not perish, but have eternal life. ¹⁷ For God did not send the Son into the world to judge the world, but that the world might be saved through Him. ¹⁸ He who believes in Him is not judged; he who does not believe has been judged already, because he has not believed in the name of the only begotten Son of God. ¹⁹ And this is the judgment, that the Light has come into the world, and

men loved the darkness rather than the Light, for their deeds were evil. ²⁰ For everyone who does evil hates the Light, and does not come to the Light lest his deeds be exposed. ²¹ But he who practices the truth comes to the Light, so that his deeds may be manifested as having been done by God."

John the Baptist's Last Witness

²² After these things Jesus and His disciples came into the land of Judea, and there He was spending time with them and baptizing. ²³ And John also was baptizing in Aenon near Salim, because there was much water there; and *people* were coming and were being baptized— ²⁴ for John had not yet been thrown into prison.

²⁵ Therefore there arose a debate between John's disciples and a Jew about purification. ²⁶ And they came to John and said to him, "Rabbi, He who was with you beyond the Jordan, to whom you have borne witness, behold, He is baptizing and all are coming to Him." ²⁷ John answered and said, "A man can receive nothing unless it has been given him from heaven. ²⁸ You yourselves are my witnesses that I said, 'I am not the Christ,' but, 'I have

been sent ahead of Him.' ²⁹ He who has the bride is the bridegroom; but the friend of the bridegroom, who stands and hears him, rejoices greatly because of the bridegroom's voice. So this joy of mine has been made full. ³⁰ He must increase, but I must decrease.

³¹ "He who comes from above is above all, he who is of the earth is from the earth and speaks of the earth. He who comes from heaven is above all. ³² What He has seen and heard, of that He bears witness; and no one receives His witness. ³³ He who has received His witness has set his seal to *this*, that God is true. ³⁴ For He whom God has sent speaks the words of God; for He gives the Spirit without measure. ³⁵ The Father loves the Son and has given all things into His hand. ³⁶ He who believes in the Son has eternal life; but he who does not obey the Son will not see life, but the wrath of God abides on him."

Jesus Goes to Galilee

4 Therefore when Jesus knew that the Pharisees had heard that Jesus was making and baptizing more disciples than John ² (although Jesus

Himself was not baptizing, but His disciples *were*), ³ He left Judea and went away again into Galilee. ⁴ And He had to pass through Samaria. ⁵ So He *came to a city of Samaria called Sychar, near the field that Jacob gave to his son Joseph; ⁶ and Jacob's well was there. So Jesus, being wearied from His journey, was sitting thus by the well. It was about the sixth hour.

Jesus and the Samaritan Woman

⁷ A woman of Samaria *came to draw water. Jesus *said to her, "Give Me a drink." ⁸ For His disciples had gone away into the city to buy food. ⁹ Therefore the Samaritan woman *said to Him, "How do You, being a Jew, ask for a drink from me, being a Samaritan woman?" (For Jews have no dealings with Samaritans.) ¹⁰ Jesus answered and said to her, "If you knew the gift of God, and who it is who says to you, 'Give Me a drink,' you would have asked Him, and He would have given you living water." ¹¹ She *said to Him, "Sir, You have nothing to draw with and the well is deep. Where then do You get that living water? ¹² Are You greater than our father Jacob, who gave us this well, and

drank of it himself and his sons and his cattle?" ¹³ Jesus answered and said to her, "Everyone who drinks of this water will thirst again; ¹⁴ but whoever drinks of the water that I will give him will never thirst—ever; but the water that I will give him will become in him a well of water springing up to eternal life."

¹⁵ The woman *said to Him, "Sir, give me this water, so I will not be thirsty nor come *back* here to draw." ¹⁶ He *said to her, "Go, call your husband and come *back* here." ¹⁷ The woman answered and said, "I have no husband." Jesus *said to her, "You have correctly said, 'I have no husband'; ¹⁸ for you had five husbands, and the one you now have is not your husband; this you have said truly." ¹⁹ The woman *said to Him, "Sir, I see that You are a prophet. ²⁰ Our fathers worshiped on this mountain, and you *people* say that in Jerusalem is the place where men ought to worship." ²¹ Jesus *said to her, "Woman, believe Me, an hour is coming when neither in this mountain nor in Jerusalem will you worship the Father. ²² You worship what you do not know; we worship what we know, for salvation is from the Jews. ²³ But an hour is

coming, and now is, when the true worshipers will worship the Father in spirit and truth; for such people the Father seeks to be His worshipers. ²⁴ God is spirit, and those who worship Him must worship in spirit and truth." ²⁵ The woman *said to Him, "I know that Messiah is coming (He who is called Christ); when He comes, He will declare all things to us." ²⁶ Jesus *said to her, "I who speak to you am *He.*"

²⁷ And at this point His disciples came, and they were marveling that He was speaking with a woman, yet no one said, "What do You seek?" or, "Why are You speaking with her?" ²⁸ So the woman left her water jar, and went into the city and *said to the men, ²⁹ "Come, see a man who told me all the things that I *have* done; is this not the Christ?" ³⁰ They went out of the city, and were coming to Him.

³¹ Meanwhile the disciples were urging Him, saying, "Rabbi, eat." ³² But He said to them, "I have food to eat that you do not know about." ³³ So the disciples were saying to one another, "Has anyone brought Him *anything* to eat?" ³⁴ Jesus *said to them, "My food is to do the will of Him who

sent Me and to finish His work. ³⁵ Do you not say, 'There are yet four months, and *then* comes the harvest'? Behold, I say to you, lift up your eyes and look on the fields, that they are white for harvest. ³⁶ Even now he who reaps is receiving wages and is gathering fruit for life eternal; so that he who sows and he who reaps may rejoice together. ³⁷ For in this *case* the saying is true, 'One sows and another reaps.' ³⁸ I sent you to reap that for which you have not labored; others have labored and you have entered into their labor."

Many Samaritans Believe

³⁹ From that city many of the Samaritans believed in Him because of the word of the woman who bore witness, "He told me all the things that I *have* done." ⁴⁰ So when the Samaritans came to Jesus, they were asking Him to stay with them; and He stayed there two days. ⁴¹ And many more believed because of His word; ⁴² and they were saying to the woman, "It is no longer because of what you said that we believe, for we have heard for ourselves and know that this One is truly the Savior of the world."

⁴³ And after the two days He went from there into Galilee. ⁴⁴ For Jesus Himself bore witness that a prophet has no honor in his own country. ⁴⁵ So when He came to Galilee, the Galileans received Him, having seen all the things that He did in Jerusalem at the feast; for they themselves also went to the feast.

Jesus Heals a Royal Official's Son

⁴⁶ Then He came again to Cana of Galilee where He had made the water wine. And there was a royal official whose son was sick at Capernaum. ⁴⁷ When he heard that Jesus had come out of Judea into Galilee, he went to Him and was asking *Him* to come down and heal his son; for he was about to die. ⁴⁸ So Jesus said to him, "Unless you *people* see signs and wonders, you will never believe." ⁴⁹ The royal official *said to Him, "Sir, come down before my child dies." ⁵⁰ Jesus *said to him, "Go; your son lives." The man believed the word that Jesus spoke to him and started on his way. ⁵¹ And while he was still going down, his slaves met him, saying that his son was alive. ⁵² So he inquired of them the hour when he began to

get better. Then they said to him, "Yesterday at the seventh hour the fever left him." ⁵³ So the father knew that *it was* at that hour in which Jesus said to him, "Your son lives"; and he himself believed and his whole household. ⁵⁴ This is again a second sign that Jesus did when He had come out of Judea into Galilee.

The Healing at Bethesda

5 After these things there was a feast of the Jews, and Jesus went up to Jerusalem.

² Now there is in Jerusalem by the sheep *gate* a pool, which is called in Hebrew Bethesda, having five porticoes. ³ In these lay a multitude of those who were sick, blind, lame, and withered, [waiting for the moving of the waters; ⁴ for an angel of the Lord went down at certain seasons into the pool and stirred up the water; whoever then first, after the stirring up of the water, stepped in was made well from whatever sickness with which he was afflicted.] ⁵ And a man was there who had been sick for thirty-eight years. ⁶ When Jesus saw him lying *there* and knew that he had already been *sick* a long time, He *said to him, "Do you

wish to get well?" ⁷ The sick man answered Him, "Sir, I have no man to put me into the pool when the water is stirred up, but while I am coming, another steps down before me." ⁸ Jesus *said to him, "Get up, pick up your mat and walk." ⁹ And immediately the man became well, and picked up his mat and *began to* walk.

Now it was the Sabbath on that day. ¹⁰ So the Jews were saying to the man who had been healed, "It is the Sabbath, and it is not lawful for you to carry your mat." ¹¹ But he answered them, "He who made me well was the one who said to me, 'Pick up your mat and walk.' " ¹² They asked him, "Who is the man who said to you, 'Pick up *your mat* and walk'?" ¹³ But the man who was healed did not know who it was, for Jesus had slipped away while there was a crowd in *that* place. ¹⁴ Afterward Jesus *found him in the temple and said to him, "Behold, you have become well; do not sin anymore, so that nothing worse happens to you." ¹⁵ The man went away, and disclosed to the Jews that it was Jesus who had made him well. ¹⁶ And for this reason the Jews were persecuting Jesus, because He was doing these things on the Sabbath. ⁱ⁷ But He answered them, "My Father is working until now, and I Myself am working."

Jesus' Equality with the Father

¹⁸ For this reason therefore the Jews were seeking all the more to kill Him, because He not only was breaking the Sabbath, but also was calling God His own Father, making Himself equal with God.

¹⁹ Therefore Jesus answered and was saying to them, "Truly, truly, I say to you, the Son can do nothing from Himself, unless *it is* something He sees the Father doing; for whatever the Father does, these things the Son also does in the same manner. ²⁰ For the Father loves the Son, and shows Him all things that He Himself is doing; and *the Father* will show Him greater works than these, so that you will marvel. ²¹ For just as the Father raises the dead and gives *them* life, even so the Son also gives life to whom He wishes. ²² For not even the Father judges anyone, but He has given all judgment to the Son, ²³ so that all will honor the Son even as they honor the Father. He who does not honor the Son does not honor the Father who sent Him.

[24] "Truly, truly, I say to you, he who hears My word, and believes Him who sent Me, has eternal life, and does not come into judgment, but has passed out of death into life.

Two Resurrections

[25] Truly, truly, I say to you, an hour is coming and now is, when the dead will hear the voice of the Son of God, and those who hear will live. [26] For just as the Father has life in Himself, even so He gave to the Son also to have life in Himself; [27] and He gave Him authority to execute judgment, because He is the Son of Man. [28] Do not marvel at this; for an hour is coming, in which all who are in the tombs will hear His voice, [29] and will come forth; those who did the good deeds to a resurrection of life, those who committed the evil deeds to a resurrection of judgment.

[30] "I can do nothing from Myself. As I hear, I judge; and My judgment is righteous, because I do not seek My own will, but the will of Him who sent Me.

[31] "If I *alone* bear witness about Myself, My witness is not true. [32] There is another who bears

witness about Me, and I know that the witness which He gives about Me is true.

Witnesses to Jesus: The Father and the Scriptures

[33] You have sent to John, and he has borne witness to the truth. [34] But the witness I receive is not from man, but I say these things so that you may be saved. [35] He was the lamp that was burning and shining and you were willing to rejoice for a while in his light. [36] But the witness I have is greater than *the witness of* John; for the works which the Father has given Me to finish—the very works that I do—bear witness about Me, that the Father has sent Me. [37] And the Father who sent Me, He has borne witness about Me. You have neither heard His voice at any time nor seen His form. [38] And you do not have His word abiding in you, for you do not believe Him whom He sent. [39] You search the Scriptures because you think that in them you have eternal life; it is these that bear witness about Me; [40] and you are unwilling to come to Me so that you may have life. [41] I do not receive glory from men; [42] but I know you, that you do not have the love of God in yourselves. [43] I have come in

My Father's name, and you do not receive Me; if another comes in his own name, you will receive him. ⁴⁴How can you believe, when you receive glory from one another and you do not seek the glory that is from the only God? ⁴⁵Do not think that I will accuse you to the Father; the one who accuses you is Moses, in whom you have set your hope. ⁴⁶For if you believed Moses, you would believe Me, for he wrote about Me. ⁴⁷But if you do not believe his writings, how will you believe My words?"

Jesus Feeds Five Thousand

6 After these things Jesus went away to the other side of the Sea of Galilee (or Tiberias). ²Now a large crowd was following Him, because they were seeing the signs which He was doing on those who were sick. ³Then Jesus went up on the mountain, and there He was sitting down with His disciples. ⁴Now the Passover, the feast of the Jews, was near. ⁵Therefore Jesus, lifting up His eyes and seeing that a large crowd was coming to Him, *said to Philip, "Where should we buy bread, so that these people may eat?" ⁶And this

He was saying to test him, for He Himself knew what He was going to do. ⁷ Philip answered Him, "Two hundred ᵇdenarii worth of bread is not sufficient for them, for everyone to receive a little." ⁸ One of His disciples, Andrew, Simon Peter's brother, *said to Him, ⁹ "There is a boy here who has five barley loaves and two fish, but what are these for so many people?" ¹⁰ Jesus said, "Have the people sit down." Now there was much grass in the place. So the men sat down, in number about five thousand. ¹¹ Jesus then took the loaves, and having given thanks, He distributed *them* to those who were seated; likewise also of the fish, as much as they wanted. ¹² And when they were filled, He *said to His disciples, "Gather up the leftover pieces so that nothing will be lost." ¹³ So they gathered them up, and filled twelve baskets with pieces of the five barley loaves left over by those who had eaten. ¹⁴ Therefore when the people saw the sign which He had done, they were saying, "This is truly the Prophet who is to come into the world."

---

b. A Roman silver coin, approx. a laborer's daily wage

Jesus Walks on the Sea

¹⁵ So Jesus, knowing that they were going to come and take Him by force to make Him king, withdrew again to the mountain by Himself alone.

¹⁶ Now when evening came, His disciples went down to the sea, ¹⁷ and after getting into a boat, they *began to* cross the sea to Capernaum. It had already become dark, and Jesus had not yet come to them. ¹⁸ And the sea *was stirred up because a strong wind was blowing. ¹⁹ Then, when they had rowed about ᶜtwenty-five or thirty stadia, they *saw Jesus walking on the sea and drawing near to the boat; and they were frightened. ²⁰ But He *said to them, "It is I; do not be afraid." ²¹ So they were willing to receive Him into the boat, and immediately the boat was at the land to which they were going.

²² On the next day, the crowd which stood on the other side of the sea saw that there was no other small boat there, except one, and that Jesus had not entered with His disciples into the boat, but *that* His disciples had gone away alone. ²³ Other small boats came from Tiberias near to the place where they ate the bread after the Lord had given

---

c. Approx. 2.8-3.5 mi. or 4.6-5.5 km; a stadion was about 607 ft. or 185 m

thanks. ²⁴ So when the crowd saw that Jesus was not there, nor His disciples, they themselves got into the small boats, and came to Capernaum seeking Jesus. ²⁵ And when they found Him on the other side of the sea, they said to Him, "Rabbi, when did You come here?"

I Am the Bread of Life

²⁶ Jesus answered them and said, "Truly, truly, I say to you, you seek Me, not because you saw signs, but because you ate of the loaves and were filled. ²⁷ Do not work for the food which perishes, but for the food which endures to eternal life, which the Son of Man will give to you, for on Him the Father, God, set His seal." ²⁸ Therefore they said to Him, "What should we do, so that we may work the works of God?" ²⁹ Jesus answered and said to them, "This is the work of God, that you believe in Him whom He has sent." ³⁰ So they said to Him, "What then do You do for a sign so that we may see, and believe You? What work do You perform? ³¹ Our fathers ate the manna in the wilderness; as it is written, 'HE GAVE THEM BREAD FROM HEAVEN TO EAT.' " ³² Jesus then said to them, "Truly, truly,

I say to you, Moses has not given you the bread from heaven, but My Father gives you the true bread from heaven. ³³ For the bread of God is that which comes down from heaven and gives life to the world." ³⁴ Then they said to Him, "Lord, always give us this bread."

³⁵ Jesus said to them, "I am the bread of life. He who comes to Me will never hunger, and he who believes in Me will never thirst. ³⁶ But I said to you that you have seen Me, and yet do not believe. ³⁷ All that the Father gives Me will come to Me, and the one who comes to Me I will never cast out. ³⁸ For I have come down from heaven, not to do My own will, but the will of Him who sent Me. ³⁹ Now this is the will of Him who sent Me, that of all that He has given Me I lose nothing, but raise it up on the last day. ⁴⁰ For this is the will of My Father, that everyone who sees the Son and believes in Him will have eternal life, and I Myself will raise him up on the last day."

Words to the Jews

⁴¹ Therefore the Jews were grumbling about Him, because He said, "I am the bread that came down

from heaven." ⁴²They were saying, "Is not this Jesus, the son of Joseph, whose father and mother we know? How does He now say, 'I have come down from heaven'?" ⁴³Jesus answered and said to them, "Stop grumbling among yourselves. ⁴⁴No one can come to Me unless the Father who sent Me draws him; and I will raise him up on the last day. ⁴⁵It is written in the prophets, 'AND THEY SHALL ALL BE TAUGHT BY GOD.' Everyone who has heard and learned from the Father comes to Me. ⁴⁶Not that anyone has seen the Father, except the One who is from God; He has seen the Father. ⁴⁷Truly, truly, I say to you, he who believes has eternal life. ⁴⁸I am the bread of life. ⁴⁹Your fathers ate the manna in the wilderness, and they died. ⁵⁰This is the bread which comes down from heaven, so that one may eat of it and not die. ⁵¹I am the living bread that came down from heaven; if anyone eats of this bread, he will live forever; and also the bread which I will give for the life of the world is My flesh."

⁵²Then the Jews *began to* argue with one another, saying, "How can this man give us *His* flesh to eat?" ⁵³So Jesus said to them, "Truly, truly, I say to you, unless you eat the flesh of the Son

of Man and drink His blood, you have no life in yourselves. ⁵⁴ He who eats My flesh and drinks My blood has eternal life, and I will raise him up on the last day. ⁵⁵ For My flesh is true food, and My blood is true drink. ⁵⁶ He who eats My flesh and drinks My blood abides in Me, and I in him. ⁵⁷ As the living Father sent Me, and I live because of the Father, so he who eats Me, he also will live because of Me. ⁵⁸ This is the bread which came down out of heaven, not as the fathers ate and died. He who eats this bread will live forever."

Words to the Disciples

⁵⁹ These things He said in the synagogue as He taught in Capernaum.

⁶⁰ Therefore many of His disciples, when they heard *this* said, "This is a difficult statement; who can listen to it?" ⁶¹ But Jesus, knowing in Himself that His disciples were grumbling at this, said to them, "Does this cause you to stumble? ⁶² *What* then if you see the Son of Man ascending to where He was before? ⁶³ The Spirit is the One who gives life; the flesh profits nothing; the words that I have spoken to you are spirit and are life. ⁶⁴ But

there are some of you who do not believe." For Jesus knew from the beginning who they were who did not believe, and who it was that would betray Him. ⁶⁵ And He was saying, "For this reason I have said to you, that no one can come to Me unless it has been granted him from the Father."

Peter Confesses Jesus Is the Christ

⁶⁶ As a result of this many of His disciples went away and were not walking with Him anymore. ⁶⁷ So Jesus said to the twelve, "Do you also want to go?" ⁶⁸ Simon Peter answered Him, "Lord, to whom shall we go? You have words of eternal life. ⁶⁹ And we have believed and have come to know that You are the Holy One of God." ⁷⁰ Jesus answered them, "Did I Myself not choose you, the twelve, and *yet* one of you is a devil?" ⁷¹ Now He was speaking of Judas *the son* of Simon Iscariot, for he, one of the twelve, was going to betray Him.

Jesus Teaches at the Feast of Booths

7 And after these things Jesus was walking in Galilee, for He was unwilling to walk in Judea because the Jews were seeking to kill Him. ² Now the feast of the Jews, the Feast of Booths, was near. ³ Therefore His brothers said to Him, "Leave here and go into Judea, so that Your disciples also may see Your works which You are doing. ⁴ For no one does anything in secret when he himself seeks to be *known* openly. If You do these things, show Yourself publicly to the world." ⁵ For not even His brothers were believing in Him. ⁶ So Jesus *said to them, "My time is not yet here, but your time is always here. ⁷ The world cannot hate you, but it hates Me because I bear witness about it, that its deeds are evil. ⁸ Go up to the feast yourselves; I am not yet going up to this feast because My time has not yet been fulfilled." ⁹ Having said these things to them, He stayed in Galilee.

¹⁰ But when His brothers had gone up to the feast, then He Himself also went up, not publicly, but as in secret. ¹¹ So the Jews were seeking Him at the feast and saying, "Where is He?" ¹² And there was much grumbling among the crowds concerning Him; some were saying, "He is a good man"; others were saying, "No, on the contrary, He leads the crowd astray." ¹³ Yet no one was speaking openly about Him for fear of the Jews.

JOHN 7:14

[14] But when it was now the middle of the feast Jesus went up into the temple, and *began to* teach. [15] The Jews then were marveling, saying, "How has this man become learned, not having been educated?" [16] So Jesus answered them and said, "My teaching is not Mine, but from Him who sent Me. [17] If anyone is willing to do His will, he will know about the teaching, whether it is of God or I speak from Myself. [18] He who speaks from himself seeks his own glory; but He who is seeking the glory of the One who sent Him, He is true, and there is no unrighteousness in Him.

[19] "Did not Moses give you the Law? And *yet* none of you does the Law. Why do you seek to kill Me?" [20] The crowd answered, "You have a demon! Who seeks to kill You?" [21] Jesus answered them, "I did one work, and you all marvel. [22] For this reason Moses has given you circumcision (not because it is from Moses, but from the fathers), and on *the* Sabbath you circumcise a man. [23] If a man receives circumcision on the Sabbath so that the Law of Moses will not be broken, are you angry with Me because I made an entire man well on *the* Sabbath? [24] Do not

judge according to appearance, but judge with righteous judgment."

²⁵ So some of the people of Jerusalem were saying, "Is this not the man whom they are seeking to kill? ²⁶ And look, He is speaking openly, and they are saying nothing to Him. Do the rulers truly know that this is the Christ? ²⁷ However, we know where this man is from; but whenever the Christ comes, no one knows where He is from." ²⁸ Then Jesus cried out in the temple, teaching and saying, "You both know Me and know where I am from; and I have not come of Myself, but He who sent Me is true, whom you do not know. ²⁹ I know Him, because I am from Him, and He sent Me." ³⁰ So they were seeking to seize Him; yet no man laid his hand on Him, because His hour had not yet come. ³¹ But many of the crowd believed in Him; and they were saying, "When the Christ comes, will He do more signs than this man did?"

³² The Pharisees heard the crowd whispering these things about Him, and the chief priests and the Pharisees sent officers to seize Him. ³³ Therefore Jesus said, "For a little while longer I

am with you, then I go to Him who sent Me. ³⁴ You will seek Me, and will not find Me; and where I am, you cannot come." ³⁵ The Jews then said to one another, "Where does this man intend to go that we will not find Him? Is He intending to go to the Dispersion among the Greeks and teach the Greeks? ³⁶ What is this statement that He said, 'You will seek Me, and will not find Me; and where I am, you cannot come'?"

³⁷ Now on the last day, the great *day* of the feast, Jesus stood and cried out, saying, "If anyone is thirsty, let him come to Me and drink. ³⁸ He who believes in Me, as the Scripture said, 'From his innermost being will flow rivers of living water.' " ³⁹ But this He spoke of the Spirit, whom those who believed in Him were going to receive; for the Spirit was not yet *given*, because Jesus was not yet glorified.

Division of People over Jesus

⁴⁰ *Some* of the crowd therefore, when they heard these words, were saying, "This truly is the Prophet." ⁴¹ Others were saying, "This is the Christ." Still others were saying, "*No*, for is the

Christ going to come from Galilee? ⁴² Has not the Scripture said that the Christ comes from the seed of David and from Bethlehem, the village where David was?" ⁴³ So a division occurred in the crowd because of Him. ⁴⁴ Some of them were wanting to seize Him, but no one laid hands on Him.

⁴⁵ The officers then came to the chief priests and Pharisees, and they said to them, "Why did you not bring Him?" ⁴⁶ The officers answered, "Never has a man spoken like this!" ⁴⁷ The Pharisees then answered them, "Have you also been led astray? ⁴⁸ Have any of the rulers or Pharisees believed in Him? ⁴⁹ But this crowd which does not know the Law is accursed." ⁵⁰ Nicodemus (he who came to Him before), being one of them, *said to them, ⁵¹ "Does our Law judge a man unless it first hears from him and knows what he is doing?" ⁵² They answered him, "Are you also from Galilee? Search and see that no prophet arises out of Galilee." ⁵³ [Everyone went to his home.

An Adulteress Forgiven

8 But Jesus went to the Mount of Olives. ² Early in the morning He came again into the temple, and all the people were coming to Him; and He sat down and *began to* teach them. ³The scribes and the Pharisees *brought a woman caught in adultery, and having set her in the center *of the court*, ⁴they *said to Him, "Teacher, this woman has been caught in adultery, in the very act. ⁵Now in the Law Moses commanded us to stone such women; what then do You say?" ⁶They were saying this, testing Him, so that they might have *evidence* to accuse Him. But Jesus stooped down and with His finger wrote on the ground. ⁷But when they persisted in asking Him, He straightened up and said to them, "Let him who is without sin among you *be the* first to throw a stone at her." ⁸Again He stooped down and wrote on the ground. ⁹When they heard it, they began *to* go out one by one, beginning with the older ones, and He was left alone, and the woman, where she was, in the center *of the court.* ¹⁰Straightening up, Jesus said to her, "Woman, where are they? Did no one condemn you?" ¹¹She said, "No one, Lord." And Jesus said, "I do not condemn you, either. Go, and from now on sin no more."]

I Am the Light of the World

¹² Then Jesus again spoke to them, saying, "I am the Light of the world; he who follows Me will never walk in the darkness, but will have the Light of life." ¹³ So the Pharisees said to Him, "You are bearing witness about Yourself; Your witness is not true." ¹⁴ Jesus answered and said to them, "Even if I bear witness about Myself, My witness is true, for I know where I came from and where I am going; but you do not know where I come from or where I am going. ¹⁵ You judge according to the flesh; I am not judging anyone. ¹⁶ But even if I do judge, My judgment is true; for I am not alone *in it*, but I and the Father who sent Me. ¹⁷ Even in your law it has been written that the witness of two men is true. ¹⁸ I am He who bears witness about Myself, and the Father who sent Me bears witness about Me." ¹⁹ So they were saying to Him, "Where is Your Father?" Jesus answered, "You know neither Me nor My Father; if you knew Me, you would know My Father also." ²⁰ These words He spoke in the treasury, as He was teaching in the temple; and no one seized Him, because His hour had not yet come.

²¹ Then He said again to them, "I am going away, and you will seek Me, and will die in your sin. Where I am going, you cannot come." ²² So the Jews were saying, "Surely He will not kill Himself, since He says, 'Where I am going, you cannot come'?" ²³ And He was saying to them, "You are from below, I am from above. You are of this world, I am not of this world. ²⁴ Therefore I said to you that you will die in your sins. For unless you believe that I am *He*, you will die in your sins." ²⁵ So they were saying to Him, "Who are You?" Jesus said to them, "What have I been saying to you *from* the beginning? ²⁶ I have many things to say and to judge concerning you, but He who sent Me is true; and the things which I heard from Him, these I am saying to the world." ²⁷ They did not know that He had been speaking to them about the Father. ²⁸ So Jesus said, "When you lift up the Son of Man, then you will know that I am *He*, and I do nothing from Myself, but I speak these things as the Father taught Me. ²⁹ And He who sent Me is with Me; He has not left Me alone, for I always do the things that are pleasing to Him." ³⁰ As He was speaking these things, many believed in Him.

The Son Will Make You Free

³¹ So Jesus was saying to those Jews who had believed Him, "If you abide in My word, *then* you are truly My disciples; ³² and you will know the truth, and the truth will make you free." ³³ They answered Him, "We are Abraham's seed and have never yet been enslaved to anyone. How is it that You say, 'You will become free'?"

³⁴ Jesus answered them, "Truly, truly, I say to you, everyone who commits sin is the slave of sin. ³⁵ And the slave does not remain in the house forever; the son does remain forever. ³⁶ So if the Son makes you free, you will be free indeed. ³⁷ I know that you are Abraham's seed; yet you are seeking to kill Me, because My word has no place in you. ³⁸ I speak the things which I have seen with *My* Father; therefore you also do the things which you heard from *your* father."

³⁹ They answered and said to Him, "Abraham is our father." Jesus *said to them, "If you are Abraham's children, you would do the deeds of Abraham. ⁴⁰ But now you are seeking to kill Me, a man who has told you the truth, which I heard from God. This Abraham did not do. ⁴¹ You are

doing the deeds of your father." They said to Him, "We were not born of sexual immorality; we have one Father: God." ⁴² Jesus said to them, "If God were your Father, you would love Me, for I proceeded forth and have come from God, for I have not even come of Myself, but He sent Me. ⁴³ Why do you not understand what I am saying? *It is* because you cannot hear My word. ⁴⁴ You are of *your* father the devil, and you want to do the desires of your father. He was a murderer from the beginning, and does not stand in the truth because there is no truth in him. Whenever he speaks a lie, he speaks from his own *nature*, for he is a liar and the father of lies. ⁴⁵ But because I speak the truth, you do not believe Me. ⁴⁶ Which one of you convicts Me of sin? If I speak truth, why do you not believe Me? ⁴⁷ He who is of God hears the words of God; for this reason you do not hear *them*, because you are not of God."

⁴⁸ The Jews answered and said to Him, "Do we not say rightly that You are a Samaritan and have a demon?" ⁴⁹ Jesus answered, "I do not have a demon, but I honor My Father, and you dishonor Me. ⁵⁰ But I do not seek My glory; there is One who seeks and

judges. ⁵¹Truly, truly, I say to you, if anyone keeps My word he will never see death—ever." ⁵²The Jews said to Him, "Now we know that You have a demon. Abraham died, and the prophets *also*; and You say, 'If anyone keeps My word, he will never taste of death—ever.' ⁵³Surely You are not greater than our father Abraham who died? The prophets died too; whom do You make Yourself out *to be*?" ⁵⁴Jesus answered, "If I glorify Myself, My glory is nothing; it is My Father who glorifies Me, of whom you say, 'He is our God'; ⁵⁵and you have not known Him, but I know Him; and if I say that I do not know Him, I will be a liar like you, but I do know Him and keep His word. ⁵⁶Your father Abraham rejoiced to see My day, and he saw *it* and was glad." ⁵⁷So the Jews said to Him, "You are not yet fifty years old, and have You seen Abraham?" ⁵⁸Jesus said to them, "Truly, truly, I say to you, before Abraham was, I am." ⁵⁹Therefore they picked up stones to throw at Him, but Jesus hid Himself and went out of the temple.

Jesus Heals a Man Born Blind

9 As He passed by, He saw a man blind from birth. ²And His disciples asked Him, saying,

"Rabbi, who sinned, this man or his parents, that he would be born blind?" ³Jesus answered, "Neither this man nor his parents sinned, but *this was* so that the works of God might be manifested in him. ⁴We must work the works of Him who sent Me as long as it is day; night is coming when no one can work. ⁵While I am in the world, I am the light of the world." ⁶When He had said this, He spat on the ground, made clay of the saliva, and rubbed the clay on his eyes, ⁷and said to him, "Go, wash in the pool of Siloam" (which is translated, Sent). So he went away and washed, and came *back* seeing. ⁸Therefore the neighbors, and those who previously saw him as a beggar, were saying, "Is not this the one who used to sit and beg?" ⁹Others were saying, "This is he," *still* others were saying, "No, but he is like him." He kept saying, "I am the one." ¹⁰So they were saying to him, "How then were your eyes opened?" ¹¹He answered, "The man who is called Jesus made clay, and rubbed my eyes, and said to me, 'Go to Siloam and wash'; so when I went away and washed, I received sight." ¹²And they said to him, "Where is He?" He *said, "I do not know."

Controversy over the Man Born Blind

¹³ They *brought to the Pharisees the man who was formerly blind. ¹⁴ Now it was a Sabbath on the day when Jesus made the clay and opened his eyes. ¹⁵ So the Pharisees also were asking him again how he received his sight. And he said to them, "He applied clay to my eyes, and I washed, and I see." ¹⁶ So then some of the Pharisees were saying, "This man is not from God, because He does not keep the Sabbath." But others were saying, "How can a sinful man do such signs?" And there was a division among them. ¹⁷ Therefore, they *said to the blind man again, "What do you say about Him, since He opened your eyes?" And he said, "He is a prophet."

¹⁸ Then, the Jews did not believe *it* of him that he was blind and had received sight, until they called the parents of the very one who had received his sight, ¹⁹ and questioned them, saying, "Is this your son, who you say was born blind? Then how does he now see?" ²⁰ So his parents answered and said, "We know that this is our son, and that he was born blind; ²¹ but how he now sees, we do not know; or who opened his eyes, we do not know.

Ask him; he is of age, he will speak for himself." ²² His parents said this because they were afraid of the Jews; for the Jews had already agreed that if anyone confessed Him to be Christ, he was to be put out of the synagogue. ²³ For this reason his parents said, "He is of age; ask him."

²⁴ Therefore, a second time they called the man who had been blind, and said to him, "Give glory to God; we know that this man is a sinner." ²⁵ He then answered, "Whether He is a sinner, I do not know; one thing I do know, that though I was blind, now I see." ²⁶ So they said to him, "What did He do to you? How did He open your eyes?" ²⁷ He answered them, "I told you already and you did not listen. Why do you want to listen again? Do you want to become His disciples too?" ²⁸ And they reviled him and said, "You are His disciple, but we are disciples of Moses. ²⁹ We know that God has spoken to Moses, but as for this man, we do not know where He is from." ³⁰ The man answered and said to them, "Well, here is a marvelous thing, that you do not know where He is from, and He opened my eyes. ³¹ We know that God does not listen to sinners; but if anyone is God-fearing and

does His will, He listens to him. ³² Since the beginning of time it has never been heard that anyone opened the eyes of a person born blind. ³³ If this man were not from God, He could do nothing." ³⁴ They answered and said to him, "You were born entirely in sins, and are you teaching us?" So they put him out.

Jesus Affirms His Deity

³⁵ Jesus heard that they had put him out, and after finding him, He said, "Do you believe in the Son of Man?" ³⁶ He answered and said, "Who is He, Lord, that I may believe in Him?" ³⁷ Jesus said to him, "You have both seen Him, and He is the one who is talking with you." ³⁸ And he said, "Lord, I believe." And he worshiped Him. ³⁹ And Jesus said, "For judgment I came into this world, so that those who do not see may see, and that those who see may become blind." ⁴⁰ Some of the Pharisees who were with Him heard these things and said to Him, "Are we blind too?" ⁴¹ Jesus said to them, "If you were blind, you would have no sin; but now *that* you say, 'We see,' your sin remains.

I Am the Good Shepherd

10 "Truly, truly, I say to you, he who does not enter by the door into the fold of the sheep, but climbs up some other way, he is a thief and a robber. ² But he who enters by the door is a shepherd of the sheep. ³ To him the doorkeeper opens, and the sheep hear his voice, and he calls his own sheep by name and leads them out. ⁴ When he brings all his own out, he goes ahead of them, and the sheep follow him because they know his voice. ⁵ A stranger they will never follow, but will flee from him, because they do not know the voice of strangers." ⁶ This figure of speech Jesus spoke to them, but they did not understand what those things were which He had been saying to them.

⁷ So Jesus said to them again, "Truly, truly, I say to you, I am the door of the sheep. ⁸ All who came before Me are thieves and robbers, but the sheep did not hear them. ⁹ I am the door; if anyone enters through Me, he will be saved, and will go in and out and find pasture. ¹⁰ The thief comes only to steal and kill and destroy; I came that they may have life, and have *it* abundantly.

¹¹ "I am the good shepherd; the good shepherd lays down His life for the sheep. ¹² He who is a hired hand, and not a shepherd, who is not the owner of the sheep, sees the wolf coming, and leaves the sheep and flees—and the wolf snatches and scatters them— ¹³ because he is a hired hand and is not concerned about the sheep. ¹⁴ I am the good shepherd, and I know My own and My own know Me, ¹⁵ even as the Father knows Me and I know the Father; and I lay down My life for the sheep. ¹⁶ And I have other sheep, which are not from this fold; I must bring them also, and they will hear My voice; and they will become one flock *with* one shepherd. ¹⁷ For this reason the Father loves Me, because I lay down My life so that I may take it again. ¹⁸ No one takes it away from Me, but from Myself, I lay it down. I have authority to lay it down, and I have authority to take it up again. This commandment I received from My Father."

¹⁹ A division occurred again among the Jews because of these words. ²⁰ And many of them were saying, "He has a demon and is insane. Why do you listen to Him?" ²¹ Others were

saying, "These are not the words of someone demon-possessed. Can a demon open the eyes of the blind?"

I and the Father Are One

²² At that time the Feast of the Dedication took place at Jerusalem; ²³ it was winter, and Jesus was walking in the temple in the Portico of Solomon. ²⁴ The Jews then gathered around Him, and were saying to Him, "How long will You keep us in suspense? If You are the Christ, tell us openly." ²⁵ Jesus answered them, "I told you, and you do not believe; the works that I do in My Father's name, these bear witness of Me. ²⁶ But you do not believe because you are not of My sheep. ²⁷ My sheep hear My voice, and I know them, and they follow Me; ²⁸ and I give eternal life to them, and they will never perish—ever; and no one will snatch them out of My hand. ²⁹ My Father, who has given *them* to Me, is greater than all; and no one is able to snatch *them* out of the Father's hand. ³⁰ I and the Father are one."

³¹ The Jews picked up stones again to stone Him. ³² Jesus answered them, "I showed you

many good works from the Father; for which of them are you stoning Me?" ³³ The Jews answered Him, "For a good work we do not stone You, but for blasphemy; and because You, being a man, make Yourself God." ³⁴ Jesus answered them, "Has it not been written in your Law, 'I SAID, YOU ARE GODS'? ³⁵ If he called them gods, to whom the word of God came (and the Scripture cannot be broken), ³⁶ do you say of Him, whom the Father sanctified and sent into the world, 'You are blaspheming,' because I said, 'I am the Son of God'? ³⁷ If I do not do the works of My Father, do not believe Me; ³⁸ but if I do them, though you do not believe Me, believe the works, so that you may know and continue knowing that the Father is in Me, and I in the Father." ³⁹ Therefore they were seeking again to seize Him, and He eluded their grasp.

⁴⁰ And He went away again beyond the Jordan to the place where John was first baptizing, and He was staying there. ⁴¹ And many came to Him and were saying, "While John did no sign, yet everything John said about this man was true." ⁴² And many believed in Him there.

JOHN 11:1

The Death and Resurrection of Lazarus

11 Now a certain man was sick, Lazarus from Bethany, the village of Mary and her sister Martha. ² And it was *the* Mary who anointed the Lord with perfume, and wiped His feet with her hair, whose brother Lazarus was sick. ³ So the sisters sent to Him, saying, "Lord, behold, he whom You love is sick." ⁴ But when Jesus heard *this*, He said, "This sickness is not to end in death, but is for the glory of God, so that the Son of God may be glorified by it." ⁵ Now Jesus loved Martha and her sister and Lazarus. ⁶ So when He heard that he was sick, He then stayed two days in the place where He was. ⁷ Then after this He *said to the disciples, "Let us go to Judea again." ⁸ The disciples *said to Him, "Rabbi, the Jews were just now seeking to stone You, and are You going there again?" ⁹ Jesus answered, "Are there not twelve hours in the day? If anyone walks in the day, he does not stumble, because he sees the light of this world. ¹⁰ But if anyone walks in the night, he stumbles, because the light is not in him." ¹¹ He said these things, and after that He *said to them, "Our friend Lazarus has fallen asleep; but I go, so that I may awaken him." ¹² The disciples then said to Him, "Lord, if he has fallen asleep, he will be saved *from his sickness*." ¹³ Now Jesus had spoken of his death, but they thought that He was speaking of actual sleep. ¹⁴ So Jesus then said to them plainly, "Lazarus is dead, ¹⁵ and I am glad for your sakes that I was not there, so that you may believe; but let us go to him." ¹⁶ Therefore Thomas, who is called Didymus, said to *his* fellow disciples, "Let us also go, so that we may die with Him."

¹⁷ So when Jesus came, He found that he had already been in the tomb four days. ¹⁸ Now Bethany was near Jerusalem, about ᵈfifteen stadia away; ¹⁹ and many of the Jews had come to Martha and Mary, to console them about their brother. ²⁰ Martha therefore, when she heard that Jesus was coming, went to meet Him, but Mary was sitting in the house. ²¹ Martha then said to Jesus, "Lord, if You had been here, my brother would not have died. ²² But even now I know that whatever You ask from God, God will give You." ²³ Jesus *said to her, "Your brother will rise again." ²⁴ Martha *said to Him, "I know that he will rise again in the

---

d. Approx. 1.7 mi. or 2.7 km, a stadion was approx. 607 ft. or 185 m

resurrection on the last day." ²⁵ Jesus said to her, "I am the resurrection and the life; he who believes in Me will live even if he dies, ²⁶ and everyone who lives and believes in Me will never die—ever. Do you believe this?" ²⁷ She *said to Him, "Yes, Lord; I have believed that You are the Christ, the Son of God, the One who comes into the world."

²⁸ And when she had said this, she went away and called Mary her sister, saying secretly, "The Teacher is here and is calling for you." ²⁹ And when she heard it, she *got up quickly and was coming to Him.

³⁰ Now Jesus had not yet come into the village, but was still in the place where Martha met Him. ³¹ Then the Jews—who were with her in the house and consoling her—when they saw that Mary rose up quickly and went out, they followed her, thinking that she was going to the tomb to cry there. ³² Therefore, when Mary came where Jesus was, she saw Him, and fell at His feet, saying to Him, "Lord, if You had been here, my brother would not have died." ³³ When Jesus therefore saw her crying, and the Jews who came with her *also* crying, He was deeply moved in spirit and was

troubled, ³⁴ and said, "Where have you laid him?" They *said to Him, "Lord, come and see." ³⁵ Jesus wept. ³⁶ So the Jews were saying, "See how He loved him!" ³⁷ But some of them said, "Could not this man, who opened the eyes of the blind man, have kept this man also from dying?"

³⁸ So Jesus, again being deeply moved within, *came to the tomb. Now it was a cave, and a stone was lying against it. ³⁹ Jesus *said, "Remove the stone." Martha, the sister of the deceased, *said to Him, "Lord, by this time he smells, for he has been *dead* four days." ⁴⁰ Jesus *said to her, "Did I not say to you that if you believe, you will see the glory of God?" ⁴¹ So they removed the stone. Then Jesus raised His eyes, and said, "Father, I thank You that You have heard Me. ⁴² And I knew that You always hear Me; but because of the crowd standing around I said this, so that they may believe that You sent Me." ⁴³ And when He had said these things, He cried out with a loud voice, "Lazarus, come forth." ⁴⁴ The man who had died came forth, bound hand and foot with wrappings, and his face was wrapped around with a cloth. Jesus *said to them, "Unbind him, and let him go."

⁴⁵ Therefore many of the Jews who came to Mary, and saw what He had done, believed in Him. ⁴⁶ But some of them went to the Pharisees and told them the things which Jesus had done.

The Leaders Plot to Kill Jesus

⁴⁷ Therefore the chief priests and the Pharisees gathered the Sanhedrin together, and were saying, "What are we doing? For this man is doing many signs. ⁴⁸ If we let Him *go on* like this, all will believe in Him, and the Romans will come and take away both our place and our nation." ⁴⁹ But one of them, Caiaphas, who was high priest that year, said to them, "You know nothing at all, ⁵⁰ nor do you take into account that it is better for you that one man should die for the people, and that the whole nation not perish." ⁵¹ Now he did not say this from himself, but being high priest that year, he prophesied that Jesus was going to die for the nation, ⁵² and not for the nation only, but in order that He might also gather together into one the children of God who are scattered abroad. ⁵³ So from that day on they planned together to kill Him.

⁵⁴ Therefore Jesus no longer continued to walk openly among the Jews, but went away from there to the region near the wilderness, into a city called Ephraim; and there He stayed with the disciples.

⁵⁵ Now the Passover of the Jews was near, and many went up to Jerusalem from the region before the Passover to purify themselves. ⁵⁶ So they were seeking Jesus, and were saying to one another as they stood in the temple, "What do you think? That He will not come to the feast at all?" ⁵⁷ Now the chief priests and the Pharisees had given orders that if anyone knew where He was, he was to report it, so that they might seize Him.

Mary Anoints Jesus with Costly Perfume

12 Jesus, therefore, six days before the Passover, came to Bethany where Lazarus was, whom Jesus had raised from the dead. ² So they made Him a supper there, and Martha was serving; and Lazarus was one of those reclining *at the table* with Him. ³ Mary then took a ᵉlitra of perfume of very costly pure nard, and anointed the feet of Jesus and wiped His feet with her hair; and

---

e. A Roman pound, approx. 12 oz. or 340 gm

the house was filled with the fragrance of the perfume. ⁴ But Judas Iscariot, one of His disciples, who was going to betray Him, *said, ⁵ "Why was this perfume not sold for three hundred denarii and given to the poor?" ⁶ Now he said this, not because he was concerned about the poor, but because he was a thief, and as he had the money box, he used to take from what was put into it. ⁷ Therefore Jesus said, "Let her alone, so that she may keep it for the day of My burial. ⁸ For you always have the poor with you, but you do not always have Me."

⁹ Then the large crowd from the Jews learned that He was there. And they came, not because of Jesus only, but that they might also see Lazarus, whom He raised from the dead. ¹⁰ But the chief priests planned to put Lazarus to death also; ¹¹ because on account of him many of the Jews were going away and were believing in Jesus.

The Triumphal Entry

¹² On the next day the large crowd who had come to the feast, when they heard that Jesus was coming to Jerusalem, ¹³ took the branches of the palm trees and went out to meet Him, and

began to shout, "Hosanna! BLESSED IS HE WHO COMES IN THE NAME OF THE LORD, even the King of Israel." ¹⁴ And Jesus, finding a young donkey, sat on it; as it is written, ¹⁵ "FEAR NOT, DAUGHTER OF ZION; BEHOLD, YOUR KING IS COMING, SEATED ON A DONKEY'S COLT." ¹⁶ These things His disciples did not understand at the first; but when Jesus was glorified, then they remembered that these things were written about Him, and that they had done these things to Him. ¹⁷ So the crowd, who was with Him when He called Lazarus out of the tomb and raised him from the dead, continued to bear witness *about Him*. ¹⁸ For this reason also the crowd went and met Him, because they heard that He had done this sign. ¹⁹ So the Pharisees said to one another, "You see that you are gaining nothing; look, the world has gone after Him."

Some Greeks Seek Jesus

²⁰ Now there were some Greeks among those who were going up to worship at the feast; ²¹ these then came to Philip, who was from Bethsaida of Galilee, and *began to* ask him, saying, "Sir,

we wish to see Jesus." ²² Philip *came and *told Andrew; Andrew and Philip *came and *told Jesus. ²³ And Jesus *answered them, saying, "The hour has come for the Son of Man to be glorified. ²⁴ Truly, truly, I say to you, unless a grain of wheat falls into the earth and dies, it remains alone; but if it dies, it bears much fruit. ²⁵ He who loves his life loses it, and he who hates his life in this world will keep it to life eternal. ²⁶ If anyone serves Me, he must follow Me; and where I am, there My servant will be also; if anyone serves Me, the Father will honor him.

The Son of Man Must Be Lifted Up

²⁷ "Now MY SOUL HAS BECOME DISMAYED; and what shall I say, 'Father, SAVE ME from this hour'? But for this purpose I came to this hour. ²⁸ Father, glorify Your name." Then a voice came from heaven: "I have both glorified it, and will glorify it again." ²⁹ So the crowd *of people* who stood by and heard it were saying that it had thundered; others were saying, "An angel has spoken to Him." ³⁰ Jesus answered and said, "This voice has not come for My sake, but for your sake. ³¹ Now

judgment is upon this world; now the ruler of this world will be cast out. ³² And I, if I am lifted up from the earth, will draw all men to Myself." ³³ But He was saying this to indicate the kind of death by which He was about to die. ³⁴ The crowd then answered Him, "We have heard from the Law that the Christ is to remain forever; and how do You say, 'The Son of Man must be lifted up'? Who is this Son of Man?" ³⁵ So Jesus said to them, "For a little while longer the Light is among you. Walk while you have the Light, so that darkness will not overtake you; he who walks in the darkness does not know where he goes. ³⁶ While you have the Light, believe in the Light, so that you may become sons of Light."

These things Jesus spoke, and He went away and hid Himself from them. ³⁷ But though He had done so many signs before them, they *still* were not believing in Him, ³⁸ so that the word of Isaiah the prophet might be fulfilled, which he spoke: "LORD, WHO HAS BELIEVED OUR REPORT? AND TO WHOM HAS THE ARM OF THE LORD BEEN REVEALED?" ³⁹ For this reason they could not believe, for Isaiah said again, ⁴⁰ "HE HAS BLINDED THEIR EYES AND HE

HARDENED THEIR HEART, LEST THEY SEE WITH THEIR EYES AND UNDERSTAND WITH THEIR HEART, AND RETURN AND I HEAL THEM." [41] These things Isaiah said because he saw His glory, and he spoke about Him. [42] Nevertheless many even of the rulers believed in Him, but because of the Pharisees they were not confessing *Him*, for fear that they would be put out of the synagogue; [43] for they loved the glory of men rather than the glory of God.

[44] And Jesus cried out and said, "He who believes in Me, does not believe in Me but in Him who sent Me. [45] And he who sees Me sees the One who sent Me. [46] I have come *as* Light into the world, so that everyone who believes in Me will not remain in darkness. [47] And if anyone hears My words and does not keep them, I do not judge him; for I did not come to judge the world, but to save the world. [48] He who rejects Me and does not receive My words, has one who judges him; the word I spoke is what will judge him on the last day. [49] For I did not speak from Myself, but the Father Himself who sent Me has given Me a commandment—what to say and what to speak. [50] And I know that His commandment is eternal

The Lord's Supper

13 Now before the Feast of the Passover, Jesus knowing that His hour had come that He would depart out of this world to the Father, having loved His own who were in the world, He loved them to the end. ² And during supper, the devil having already put into the heart of Judas Iscariot, *the son* of Simon, to betray Him, ³ *Jesus,* knowing that the Father had given all things into His hands, and that He had come forth from God and was going back to God, ⁴ *got up from supper, and *laid aside His garments; and taking a towel, He tied it around Himself.

Jesus Washes the Disciples' Feet

⁵ Then He *poured water into the washbasin, and began to wash the disciples' feet and to wipe them with the towel which He had tied around *Himself*. ⁶ So He *came to Simon Peter. He *said to Him, "Lord, are You going to wash my feet?" ⁷ Jesus answered and said to him, "What I am doing you

do not realize now, but you will understand afterwards." ⁸ Peter *said to Him, "You will never wash my feet—ever!" Jesus answered him, "If I do not wash you, you have no part with Me." ⁹ Simon Peter *said to Him, "Lord, not only my feet, but also my hands and my head." ¹⁰ Jesus *said to him, "He who has bathed needs only to wash his feet, but is completely clean; and you are clean, but not all *of you.*" ¹¹ For He knew the one who was betraying Him; for this reason He said, "Not all of you are clean."

¹² So when He had washed their feet, and taken His garments and reclined *at the table* again, He said to them, "Do you know what I have done to you? ¹³ You call Me Teacher and Lord; and you are right, for *so* I am. ¹⁴ If I then, the Lord and the Teacher, washed your feet, you also ought to wash one another's feet. ¹⁵ For I gave you an example that you also should do as I did to you. ¹⁶ Truly, truly, I say to you, a slave is not greater than his master, nor *is* one who is sent greater than the one who sent him. ¹⁷ If you know these things, you are blessed if you do them. ¹⁸ I do not speak about all of you. I know the ones I have chosen; but that

the Scripture may be fulfilled, 'HE WHO EATS MY BREAD HAS LIFTED UP HIS HEEL AGAINST ME.' [19] From now on I am telling you before *it* occurs, so that when it does occur, you may believe that I am *He*. [20] Truly, truly, I say to you, he who receives anyone I send receives Me; and he who receives Me receives Him who sent Me."

Jesus Predicts His Betrayal

[21] When Jesus had said these things, He became troubled in spirit, and bore witness and said, "Truly, truly, I say to you, that one of you will betray Me." [22] The disciples *began* looking at one another, perplexed about whom He *spoke. [23] There was reclining on Jesus' bosom one of His disciples, whom Jesus loved. [24] So Simon Peter *gestured to him to inquire, "Who is the one of whom He is speaking?" [25] He, leaning back thus on Jesus' bosom, *said to Him, "Lord, who is it?" [26] Jesus *answered, "He is the one for whom I shall dip the piece of bread and give it to him." So when He had dipped the piece of bread, He *took and *gave it to Judas, *the son* of Simon Iscariot. [27] And after the piece of bread, Satan then entered into

him. Therefore Jesus *said to him, "What you do, do quickly." ²⁸ Now no one of those reclining *at the table* knew for what purpose He had said this to him. ²⁹ For some were thinking, because Judas had the money box, that Jesus was saying to him, "Buy the things we have need of for the feast"; or else, that he should give something to the poor. ³⁰ So after receiving the piece of bread, he went out immediately. And it was night.

³¹ Therefore when he had gone out, Jesus *said, "Now is the Son of Man glorified, and God is glorified in Him; ³² if God is glorified in Him, God will also glorify Him in Himself, and will glorify Him immediately. ³³ Little children, I am with you a little while longer. You will seek Me; and as I said to the Jews, now I also say to you, 'Where I am going, you cannot come.' ³⁴ A new commandment I give to you, that you love one another, even as I have loved you, that you also love one another. ³⁵ By this all will know that you are My disciples, if you have love for one another."

³⁶ Simon Peter *said to Him, "Lord, where are You going?" Jesus answered, "Where I go, you cannot follow Me now; but you will follow later."

³⁷ Peter *said to Him, "Lord, why can I not follow You right now? I will lay down my life for You." ³⁸ Jesus *answered, "Will you lay down your life for Me? Truly, truly, I say to you, a rooster will not crow until you deny Me three times.

I Am the Way, the Truth, and the Life

14 "Do not let your heart be troubled; believe in God, believe also in Me. ² In My Father's house are many dwelling places; if it were not so, I would have told you; for I go to prepare a place for you. ³ And if I go and prepare a place for you, I will come again and receive you to Myself, that where I am, *there* you may be also. ⁴ And you know the way where I am going." ⁵ Thomas *said to Him, "Lord, we do not know where You are going. How do we know the way?" ⁶ Jesus *said to him, "I am the way, and the truth, and the life. No one comes to the Father but through Me.

Oneness with the Father

⁷ If you have come to know Me, you will know My Father also; from now on you know Him, and have seen Him."

⁸ Philip *said to Him, "Lord, show us the Father, and it is enough for us." ⁹ Jesus *said to him, "Have I been with you all so long and have you not come to know Me, Philip? He who has seen Me has seen the Father; how *can* you say, 'Show us the Father'? ¹⁰ Do you not believe that I am in the Father, and the Father is in Me? The words that I say to you I do not speak from Myself, but the Father abiding in Me does His works. ¹¹ Believe Me that I am in the Father and the Father is in Me; otherwise believe because of the works themselves. ¹² Truly, truly, I say to you, he who believes in Me, the works that I do, he will do also; and greater *works* than these he will do because I go to the Father. ¹³ Whatever you ask in My name, this will I do, so that the Father may be glorified in the Son. ¹⁴ If you ask Me anything in My name, I will do *it*.

¹⁵ "If you love Me, you will keep My commandments.

Jesus Promises the Holy Spirit
¹⁶ And I will ask the Father, and He will give you another Advocate, that He may be with you

forever; ¹⁷ the Spirit of truth, whom the world cannot receive, because it does not see Him or know Him. You know Him because He abides with you and will be in you.

¹⁸ "I will not leave you as orphans; I will come to you. ¹⁹ After a little while the world will no longer see Me, but you *will* see Me; because I live, you will live also. ²⁰ On that day you will know that I am in My Father, and you in Me, and I in you. ²¹ He who has My commandments and keeps them is the one who loves Me; and he who loves Me will be loved by My Father, and I will love him and will disclose Myself to him." ²² Judas (not Iscariot) *said to Him, "Lord, what then has happened that You are going to disclose Yourself to us and not to the world?" ²³ Jesus answered and said to him, "If anyone loves Me, he will keep My word; and My Father will love him, and We will come to him and make Our dwelling with him. ²⁴ He who does not love Me does not keep My words; and the word which you hear is not Mine, but the Father's who sent Me.

²⁵ "These things I have spoken to you while abiding with you. ²⁶ But the Advocate, the Holy Spirit, whom the Father will send in My name, He will

teach you all things, and bring to your remembrance all that I said to you. ²⁷ Peace I leave with you; My peace I give to you; not as the world gives do I give to you. Do not let your heart be troubled, nor let it be fearful. ²⁸ You heard that I said to you, 'I go away, and I will come to you.' If you loved Me, you would have rejoiced because I go to the Father, for the Father is greater than I. ²⁹ And now I have told you before it happens, so that when it happens, you may believe. ³⁰ I will not speak much more with you, for the ruler of the world is coming, and he has nothing in Me; ³¹ but so that the world may know that I love the Father, I do exactly as the Father commanded Me. Get up, let us go from here.

I Am the True Vine

15 "I am the true vine, and My Father is the vine-grower. ² Every branch in Me that does not bear fruit, He takes away; and every *branch* that bears fruit, He cleans it so that it may bear more fruit. ³ You are already clean because of the word which I have spoken to you. ⁴ Abide in Me, and I in you. As the branch cannot bear fruit from itself unless it abides in the vine, so neither *can* you unless you abide in Me. ⁵ I am the vine, you are the branches; he who abides in Me and I in him, he bears much fruit, for apart from Me you can do nothing. ⁶ If anyone does not abide in Me, he is thrown away as a branch and dries up; and they gather them, and cast them into the fire and they are burned. ⁷ If you abide in Me, and My words abide in you, ask whatever you wish, and it will be done for you. ⁸ My Father is glorified by this, that you bear much fruit, and *so* prove to be My disciples. ⁹ Just as the Father has loved Me, I have also loved you; abide in My love. ¹⁰ If you keep My commandments, you will abide in My love; just as I have kept My Father's commandments and abide in His love. ¹¹ These things I have spoken to you so that My joy may be in you, and *that* your joy may be complete.

Jesus' Commandment Is Love

¹² "This is My commandment, that you love one another, just as I have loved you. ¹³ Greater love has no one than this, that one lay down his life for his friends. ¹⁴ You are My friends if you do what I

command you. ¹⁵ No longer do I call you slaves, for the slave does not know what his master is doing; but I have called you friends, for all things that I have heard from My Father I have made known to you. ¹⁶ You did not choose Me but I chose you, and appointed you that you would go and bear fruit, and *that* your fruit would abide, so that whatever you ask of the Father in My name He may give to you. ¹⁷ This I command you, that you love one another.

If the World Hates You

¹⁸ "If the world hates you, know that it has hated Me before *it hated* you. ¹⁹ If you were of the world, the world would love its own; but because you are not of the world, but I chose you out of the world, because of this the world hates you. ²⁰ Remember the word that I said to you, 'A slave is not greater than his master.' If they persecuted Me, they will also persecute you; if they kept My word, they will keep yours also. ²¹ But all these things they will do to you for My name's sake, because they do not know the One who sent Me. ²² If I had not come and spoken to them, they would not have sin, but

now they have no excuse for their sin. ²³ He who hates Me hates My Father also. ²⁴ If I had not done among them the works which no one else did, they would not have sin; but now they have both seen and hated Me and My Father as well. ²⁵ But *this happened* to fulfill the word that is written in their Law, 'They hated Me without cause.'

²⁶ "When the Advocate comes, whom I will send to you from the Father, the Spirit of truth who proceeds from the Father, He will bear witness about Me, ²⁷ and you *will* bear witness also, because you have been with Me from the beginning.

Jesus' Warning

16 "These things I have spoken to you so that you may be kept from stumbling. ² They will put you out of the synagogue, but an hour is coming for everyone who kills you to think that he is offering service to God. ³ These things they will do because they did not know the Father or Me. ⁴ But these things I have spoken to you, so that when their hour comes, you may remember that I told you of them. These things I did not say to you at the beginning, because I was with you.

The Spirit Is Promised Again

⁵ "But now I am going to Him who sent Me; and none of you asks Me, 'Where are You going?' ⁶ But because I have said these things to you, sorrow has filled your heart. ⁷ But I tell you the truth, it is to your advantage that I go away; for if I do not go away, the Advocate will not come to you; but if I go, I will send Him to you. ⁸ And He, when He comes, will convict the world concerning sin and righteousness and judgment; ⁹ concerning sin, because they do not believe in Me; ¹⁰ and concerning righteousness, because I go to the Father and you no longer see Me; ¹¹ and concerning judgment, because the ruler of this world has been judged.

¹² "I still have many more things to say to you, but you cannot bear *them* now. ¹³ But when He, the Spirit of truth, comes, He will guide you into all the truth; for He will not speak from Himself, but whatever He hears, He will speak; and He will disclose to you what is to come. ¹⁴ He will glorify Me, for He will take of Mine and will disclose *it* to you. ¹⁵ All things that the Father has are Mine; therefore I said that He takes of Mine and will disclose *it* to you.

Sorrow Turned to Joy

[16] "A little while, and you will no longer see Me; and again a little while, and you will see Me." [17] *Some* of His disciples then said to one another, "What is this He is telling us, 'A little while, and you will not see Me; and again a little while, and you will see Me'; and, 'because I go to the Father'?" [18] So they were saying, "What is this that He says, 'A little while'? We do not know what He is talking about." [19] Jesus knew that they were wishing to question Him, and He said to them, "Are you deliberating together about this, that I said, 'A little while, and you will not see Me, and again a little while, and you will see Me'? [20] Truly, truly, I say to you, that you will cry and lament, but the world will rejoice; you will be sorrowful, but your sorrow will be turned into joy. [21] Whenever a woman is in labor she has sorrow, because her hour has come; but when she gives birth to the child, she no longer remembers the suffering because of the joy that a child has been born into the world. [22] Therefore you too have sorrow now; but I will see you again, and your heart will rejoice, and no one *will* take your joy away from you.

I Have Overcome the World

²³ And on that day you will not question Me about anything. Truly, truly, I say to you, if you ask the Father for anything in My name, He will give it to you. ²⁴ Until now you have asked for nothing in My name; ask and you will receive, so that your joy may be made complete.

²⁵ "These things I have spoken to you in figures of speech; an hour is coming when I will no longer speak to you in figures of speech, but will tell you openly of the Father. ²⁶ On that day you will ask in My name, and I do not say to you that I will request of the Father on your behalf; ²⁷ for the Father Himself loves you, because you have loved Me and have believed that I came forth from the Father. ²⁸ I came forth from the Father and have come into the world; I am leaving the world again and going to the Father."

²⁹ His disciples *said, "Behold, now You are speaking openly and are not using a figure of speech. ³⁰ Now we know that You know all things, and have no need for anyone to question You; by this we believe that You came from God." ³¹ Jesus answered them, "Do you now believe? ³² Behold,

an hour is coming, and has *already* come, for you to be scattered, each to his own *home*, and to leave Me alone; and *yet* I am not alone, because the Father is with Me. ³³ These things I have spoken to you, so that in Me you may have peace. In the world you have tribulation, but take courage; I have overcome the world."

The High Priestly Prayer

17 Jesus spoke these things; and lifting up His eyes to heaven, He said, "Father, the hour has come; glorify Your Son, that the Son may glorify You, ² even as You gave Him authority over all flesh, that to all whom You have given Him, He may give eternal life. ³ And this is eternal life, that they may know You, the only true God, and Jesus Christ whom You have sent. ⁴ I glorified You on the earth, having finished the work which You have given Me to do. ⁵ Now, Father, glorify Me together with Yourself, with the glory which I had with You before the world was.

Jesus Prays for His Disciples

⁶ "I have manifested Your name to the men

whom You gave Me out of the world; they were Yours and You gave them to Me, and they have kept Your word. ⁷Now they have come to know that everything You have given Me is from You; ⁸for the words which You gave Me I have given to them; and they received *them* and truly understood that I came forth from You, and they believed that You sent Me. ⁹I ask on their behalf; I do not ask on behalf of the world but of those whom You have given Me; for they are Yours; ¹⁰and all things that are Mine are Yours, and Yours are Mine; and I have been glorified in them. ¹¹And I am no longer in the world; and *yet* they themselves are in the world, and I come to You. Holy Father, keep them in Your name, *the name* which You have given Me, that they may be one even as We *are*. ¹²While I was with them, I was keeping them in Your name which You have given Me; and I guarded them and not one of them perished but the son of perdition, so that the Scripture would be fulfilled. ¹³But now I come to You; and these things I speak in the world so that they may have My joy made full in themselves. ¹⁴I have given them Your word; and the world has hated them, because they are not of the world, even as I am not of the world. ¹⁵ I do not ask You to take them out of the world, but to keep them from the evil one. ¹⁶ They are not of the world, even as I am not of the world. ¹⁷ Sanctify them by the truth; Your word is truth. ¹⁸ As You sent Me into the world, I also sent them into the world. ¹⁹ For their sake I sanctify Myself, that they themselves also may be sanctified in truth.

²⁰ "I do not ask on behalf of these alone, but for those also who believe in Me through their word; ²¹ that they may all be one; even as You, Father, *are* in Me and I in You, that they also may be in Us, so that the world may believe that You sent Me. ²² The glory which You have given Me I have given to them, that they may be one, just as We are one; ²³ I in them and You in Me, that they may be perfected in unity, so that the world may know that You sent Me, and loved them, even as You have loved Me. ²⁴ Father, I desire that they also, whom You have given Me, be with Me where I am, so that they may see My glory which You have given Me, for You loved Me before the foundation of the world.

⁲⁵ "O righteous Father, although the world has not known You, yet I have known You; and these have known that You sent Me; ²⁶ and I have made Your name known to them, and will make it known, so that the love with which You loved Me may be in them, and I in them."

Jesus Betrayed and Arrested

18 When Jesus had spoken these words, He went forth with His disciples to the other side of the Kidron Valley, where there was a garden, into which He entered with His disciples. ² Now Judas also, who was betraying Him, knew the place, for Jesus had often gathered there with His disciples. ³ Judas then, having received the *Roman* cohort and officers from the chief priests and the Pharisees, *came there with lanterns and torches and weapons. ⁴ So Jesus, knowing all the things that were coming upon Him, went forth and *said to them, "Whom do you seek?" ⁵ They answered Him, "Jesus the Nazarene." He *said to them, "I am *He.*" And Judas also, who was betraying Him, was standing with them. ⁶ So when He said to them, "I am *He*," they drew back and fell to the ground. ⁷Therefore He again asked them, "Whom do you seek?" And they said, "Jesus the Nazarene." ⁸Jesus answered, "I told you that I am *He*; so if you seek Me, let these go their way," ⁹in order that the word which He spoke would be fulfilled, "Of those whom You have given Me, I lost not one." ¹⁰Simon Peter then, having a sword, drew it and struck the high priest's slave, and cut off his right ear; and the slave's name was Malchus. ¹¹So Jesus said to Peter, "Put the sword into the sheath; the cup which the Father has given Me, shall I not drink it?"

Jesus Before the Priests; Peter Denies Jesus

¹²So the *Roman* cohort and the commander and the officers of the Jews, arrested Jesus and bound Him, ¹³and led Him to Annas first; for he was father-in-law of Caiaphas, who was high priest that year. ¹⁴Now Caiaphas was the one who had advised the Jews that it was better for one man to die on behalf of the people.

¹⁵And Simon Peter was following Jesus, and *so was* another disciple. Now that disciple was known to the high priest, and entered with Jesus

into the court of the high priest, ¹⁶ but Peter was standing at the door outside. So the other disciple, who was known to the high priest, went out and spoke to the doorkeeper, and brought Peter in. ¹⁷ Then the servant-girl who kept the door *said to Peter, "Are you not also *one* of this man's disciples?" He *said, "I am not." ¹⁸ Now the slaves and the officers were standing *there*, having made a charcoal fire, for it was cold and they were warming themselves; and Peter was also with them, standing and warming himself.

¹⁹ The high priest then questioned Jesus about His disciples, and about His teaching. ²⁰ Jesus answered him, "I have spoken openly to the world; I always taught in synagogues and in the temple, where all the Jews come together; and I spoke nothing in secret. ²¹ Why do you question Me? Question those who have heard what I spoke to them; behold, they know what I said." ²² And when He had said this, one of the officers standing nearby gave Jesus a slap, saying, "Is that the way You answer the high priest?" ²³ Jesus answered him, "If I have spoken wrongly, bear witness of the wrong; but if rightly, why do you strike Me?"

²⁴ So Annas sent Him bound to Caiaphas the high priest.

²⁵ Now Simon Peter was standing and warming himself. So they said to him, "You are not also *one* of His disciples, are you?" He denied *it*, and said, "I am not." ²⁶ One of the slaves of the high priest, being a relative of the one whose ear Peter cut off, *said, "Did I not see you in the garden with Him?" ²⁷ Peter then denied *it* again, and immediately a rooster crowed.

Jesus Before Pilate

²⁸ Then they *led Jesus from Caiaphas into the Praetorium, and it was early; and they themselves did not enter into the Praetorium so that they would not be defiled, but might eat the Passover. ²⁹ Therefore Pilate went out to them and *said, "What accusation do you bring against this man?" ³⁰ They answered and said to him, "If this man were not an evildoer, we would not have delivered Him to you." ³¹ So Pilate said to them, "Take Him yourselves, and judge Him according to your law." The Jews said to him, "It is not lawful for us to put anyone to death," ³² in order

that the word of Jesus which He spoke would be fulfilled, signifying by what kind of death He was about to die.

³³ Therefore Pilate entered again into the Praetorium, and summoned Jesus and said to Him, "Are You the King of the Jews?" ³⁴ Jesus answered, "Are you saying this from yourself, or did others tell you about Me?" ³⁵ Pilate answered, "Am I a Jew? Your own nation and the chief priests delivered You to me; what did You do?" ³⁶ Jesus answered, "My kingdom is not of this world. If My kingdom were of this world, then My servants would be fighting so that I would not be delivered over to the Jews; but as it is, My kingdom is not from here." ³⁷ Therefore Pilate said to Him, "So You are a king?" Jesus answered, "You yourself said I am a king. For this I have been born, and for this I have come into the world, to bear witness to the truth. Everyone who is of the truth hears My voice." ³⁸ Pilate *said to Him, "What is truth?"

And when he had said this, he went out again to the Jews and *said to them, "I find no guilt in Him. ³⁹ But you have a custom that I release someone for you at the Passover; do you wish then that I release for you the King of the Jews?" ⁴⁰ So they cried out again, saying, "Not this man, but Barabbas." Now Barabbas was a robber.

Jesus Flogged and Rejected as King

19 Pilate then took Jesus and flogged Him. ² And when the soldiers twisted together a crown of thorns, they put it on His head, and put a purple robe on Him; ³ and they were coming to Him and saying, "Hail, King of the Jews!" and were giving Him slaps *in the face.* ⁴ And Pilate came out again and *said to them, "Behold, I am bringing Him out to you so that you may know that I find no guilt in Him." ⁵ Jesus then came out, wearing the crown of thorns and the purple robe. *Pilate* *said to them, "Behold, the man!" ⁶ So when the chief priests and the officers saw Him, they cried out saying, "Crucify, crucify!" Pilate *said to them, "Take Him yourselves and crucify Him, for I find no guilt in Him." ⁷ The Jews answered him, "We have a law, and by that law He ought to die because He made Himself out *to be* the Son of God."

⁸ Therefore when Pilate heard this statement,

he became more afraid; ⁹ and he entered into the Praetorium again and *said to Jesus, "Where are You from?" But Jesus gave him no answer. ¹⁰ So Pilate *said to Him, "You do not speak to me? Do You not know that I have authority to release You, and I have authority to crucify You?" ¹¹ Jesus answered, "You would have no authority over Me, unless it had been given you from above; for this reason he who delivered Me to you has *the* greater sin." ¹² As a result of this Pilate kept seeking to release Him, but the Jews cried out saying, "If you release this man, you are no friend of Caesar; everyone who makes himself *to be* a king opposes Caesar."

¹³ Therefore when Pilate heard these words, he brought Jesus out, and sat down on the judgment seat at a place called The Stone Pavement, but in Hebrew, Gabbatha. ¹⁴ Now it was the day of Preparation for the Passover; it was about the sixth hour. And he *said to the Jews, "Behold, your King!" ¹⁵ So they cried out, "Away with *Him*! Away with *Him*! Crucify Him!" Pilate *said to them, "Shall I crucify your King?" The chief priests answered, "We have no king but Caesar."

The Crucifixion

16 So he then delivered Him over to them to be crucified.

17 They took Jesus, therefore, and He went out, bearing His own cross, to the place called the Place of a Skull, which is called in Hebrew, Golgotha. 18 There they crucified Him, and with Him two other men, one on either side, and Jesus in between. 19 And Pilate also wrote an inscription and put it on the cross. It was written, "JESUS THE NAZARENE, THE KING OF THE JEWS." 20 Therefore many of the Jews read this inscription, for the place where Jesus was crucified was near the city; and it was written in Hebrew, Latin, *and* in Greek. 21 So the chief priests of the Jews were saying to Pilate, "Do not write, 'The King of the Jews;' but that He said, 'I am King of the Jews.'" 22 Pilate answered, "What I have written I have written."

23 Then the soldiers, when they had crucified Jesus, took His garments and made four parts, a part to each soldier and *also* His tunic; now that tunic was seamless, woven in one piece from the top. 24 So they said to one another, "Let us not

tear it, but cast lots for it, *to decide* whose it shall be;" *this was* in order that the Scripture would be fulfilled: "THEY DIVIDED MY GARMENTS AMONG THEM, AND FOR MY CLOTHING THEY CAST LOTS." [25] Therefore the soldiers did these things.

But standing by the cross of Jesus were His mother, and His mother's sister, Mary the *wife* of Clopas, and Mary Magdalene. [26] When Jesus then saw His mother, and the disciple whom He loved standing nearby, He *said to His mother, "Woman, behold, your son!" [27] Then He *said to the disciple, "Behold, your mother!" From that hour the disciple took her into his *home*.

Scripture Fulfilled—It Is Finished

[28] After this, Jesus, knowing that all things had already been finished, in order to finish the Scripture, *said, "I am thirsty." [29] A jar full of sour wine was standing there; so they put a sponge full of the sour wine upon *a branch of* hyssop and brought it up to His mouth. [30] Therefore when Jesus had received the sour wine, He said, "It is finished!" And bowing His head, He gave up His spirit.

³¹ Then the Jews, because it was the day of Preparation, so that the bodies would not remain on the cross on the Sabbath (for that Sabbath was a high day), asked Pilate that their legs might be broken, and *that* they might be taken away. ³² So the soldiers came, and broke the legs of the first man and of the other who was crucified with Him; ³³ but coming to Jesus, when they saw that He was already dead, they did not break His legs. ³⁴ But one of the soldiers pierced His side with a spear, and immediately blood and water came out. ³⁵ And he who has seen has borne witness, and his witness is true; and he knows that he is telling the truth, so that you also may believe. ³⁶ For these things came to pass in order that the Scripture would be fulfilled, "NOT A BONE OF HIM SHALL BE BROKEN." ³⁷ And again another Scripture says, "THEY SHALL LOOK ON HIM WHOM THEY PIERCED."

Jesus Is Buried

³⁸ Now after these things Joseph of Arimathea, being a disciple of Jesus, but secretly because of his fear of the Jews, asked Pilate that he might take away the body of Jesus; and Pilate granted

permission. So he came and took away His body. ³⁹ And Nicodemus, who had first come to Him by night, also came, bringing a mixture of myrrh and aloes, *weighing* about one hundred litras. ⁴⁰ So they took the body of Jesus and bound it in linen wrappings with the spices, as is the burial custom of the Jews. ⁴¹ Now in the place where He was crucified there was a garden, and in the garden a new tomb in which no one had yet been laid. ⁴² Therefore because of the Jewish day of Preparation, since the tomb was nearby, they laid Jesus there.

The Empty Tomb

20 Now on the first *day* of the week, Mary Magdalene *came early to the tomb, while it *was still dark, and *saw the stone *already* taken away from the tomb. ² So she *ran and *came to Simon Peter and to the other disciple whom Jesus loved, and *said to them, "They have taken away the Lord out of the tomb, and we do not know where they have laid Him." ³ So Peter and the other disciple went forth, and they were going to the tomb. ⁴ And the two were running together; and the other disciple ran ahead faster than Peter and came to the tomb first; ⁵ and stooping and looking in, he *saw the linen wrappings lying *there*; but he did not go in. ⁶ And so Simon Peter also *came, following him, and entered the tomb; and he *saw the linen wrappings lying there, ⁷ and the face-cloth which had been on His head, not lying with the linen wrappings, but folded up in a place by itself. ⁸ So the other disciple who had first come to the tomb then also entered, and he saw and believed. ⁹ For as yet they did not understand the Scripture, that He must rise again from the dead. ¹⁰ So the disciples went away again to where they were staying.

Jesus Appears to Mary Magdalene

¹¹ But Mary was standing outside the tomb crying; and so, as she was crying, she stooped to look into the tomb; ¹² and she *saw two angels in white sitting, one at the head and one at the feet, where the body of Jesus had been lying. ¹³ And they *said to her, "Woman, why are you crying?" She *said to them, "Because they have taken away my Lord, and I do not know where they have laid Him." ¹⁴ When she had said this, she turned around and *saw Jesus standing *there*, and did not know that

JOHN 20:15

it was Jesus. ¹⁵ Jesus *said to her, "Woman, why are you crying? Whom are you seeking?" Thinking Him to be the gardener, she *said to Him, "Sir, if you have carried Him away, tell me where you have laid Him, and I will take Him away." ¹⁶ Jesus *said to her, "Mary!" She turned and *said to Him in Hebrew, "Rabboni!" (which means, Teacher). ¹⁷ Jesus *said to her, "Stop clinging to Me, for I have not yet ascended to the Father; but go to My brothers and say to them, 'I ascend to My Father and your Father, and My God and your God.' " ¹⁸ Mary Magdalene *came, announcing to the disciples, "I have seen the Lord," and *that* He had said these things to her.

Jesus Appears to His Disciples

¹⁹ So while it was evening on that day, the first *day* of the week, and while the doors were shut where the disciples were, for fear of the Jews, Jesus came and stood in their midst and *said to them, "Peace *be* with you." ²⁰ And when He had said this, He showed them both His hands and His side. The disciples then rejoiced when they saw the Lord. ²¹ So Jesus said to them again, "Peace

be with you; as the Father has sent Me, I also send you." ²² And when He had said this, He breathed on *them* and *said to them, "Receive the Holy Spirit. ²³ If you forgive the sins of any, *their sins* have been forgiven them; if you retain the *sins* of any, they have been retained."

²⁴ But Thomas, one of the twelve, called Didymus, was not with them when Jesus came. ²⁵ So the other disciples were saying to him, "We have seen the Lord!" But he said to them, "Unless I see in His hands the imprint of the nails, and put my finger into the place of the nails, and put my hand into His side, I will not believe."

²⁶ And after eight days His disciples were again inside, and Thomas with them. Jesus *came, the doors having been shut, and stood in their midst and said, "Peace *be* with you." ²⁷ Then He *said to Thomas, "Bring your finger here, and see My hands; and bring your hand *here* and put it into My side; and do not be unbelieving, but believing." ²⁸ Thomas answered and said to Him, "My Lord and my God!" ²⁹ Jesus *said to him, "Because you have seen Me, have you believed? Blessed *are* those who did not see, and *yet* believed."

Why This Gospel Was Written

30 Therefore many other signs Jesus also did in the presence of the disciples, which are not written in this book; 31 but these have been written so that you may believe that Jesus is the Christ, the Son of God; and that believing you may have life in His name.

Jesus Appears at the Sea of Galilee

21 After these things Jesus manifested Himself again to the disciples at the Sea of Tiberias, and He manifested *Himself* in this way. 2 Simon Peter, and Thomas called Didymus, and Nathanael of Cana in Galilee, and the *sons* of Zebedee, and two others of His disciples were together. 3 Simon Peter *said to them, "I am going fishing." They *said to him, "We will also come with you." They went out and got into the boat; and that night they caught nothing.

4 But when the day was now breaking, Jesus stood on the beach; yet the disciples did not know that it was Jesus. 5 So Jesus *said to them, "Children, do you have any fish?" They answered Him, "No." 6 And He said to them, "Cast the net on

the right side of the boat and you will find *some*." So they cast, and then they were not able to haul it in because of the great number of fish. ⁷ Therefore that disciple whom Jesus loved *said to Peter, "It is the Lord." So when Simon Peter heard that it was the Lord, he put his outer garment on (for he was stripped *for work*), and cast himself into the sea. ⁸ But the other disciples came in the little boat, for they were not far from the land, but about ᶠtwo hundred cubits away, dragging the net *full* of fish.

⁹ So when they got out on the land, they *saw a charcoal fire in place and fish placed on it, and bread. ¹⁰ Jesus *said to them, "Bring some of the fish which you have now caught." ¹¹ Simon Peter went up and drew the net to land, full of large fish, 153; and although there were so many, the net was not torn.

Jesus Provides Breakfast

¹² Jesus *said to them, "Come, have breakfast." None of the disciples dared to question Him, "Who are You?" knowing that it was the Lord. ¹³ Jesus *came and *took the bread and *gave *it* to

---
f. Approx. 98 yds. or 91 m, a cubit was approx. 18 in. or 45 cm

them, and the fish likewise. ¹⁴ This is now the third time that Jesus was manifested to the disciples, after He was raised from the dead.

Peter's Restoration and Commission

¹⁵ So when they had finished breakfast, Jesus *said to Simon Peter, "Simon, *son* of John, do you love Me more than these?" He *said to Him, "Yes, Lord; You know that I love You." He *said to him, "Tend My lambs." ¹⁶ He *said to him again a second time, "Simon, *son* of John, do you love Me?" He *said to Him, "Yes, Lord; You know that I love You." He *said to him, "Shepherd My sheep." ¹⁷ He *said to him the third time, "Simon, *son* of John, do you love Me?" Peter was grieved because He said to him the third time, "Do you love Me?" And he said to Him, "Lord, You know all things; You know that I love You." Jesus *said to him, "Tend My sheep. ¹⁸ Truly, truly, I say to you, when you were younger, you used to gird yourself and walk wherever you wished; but when you grow old, you will stretch out your hands and someone else will gird you, and bring you where you do not wish to *go.*" ¹⁹ Now this He said, signifying by what kind

of death he would glorify God. And when He had spoken this, He *said to him, "Follow Me!"

Jesus' Command to Follow Him

²⁰ Peter, turning around, *saw the disciple whom Jesus loved following *them*; the one who also had leaned back on His bosom at the supper and said, "Lord, who is the one who betrays You?" ²¹ So Peter seeing him *said to Jesus, "Lord, and what about this man?" ²² Jesus *said to him, "If I want him to remain until I come, what *is that* to you? You follow Me!" ²³ Therefore this saying went out among the brothers that this disciple would not die; yet Jesus did not say to him that he would not die, but *only*, "If I want him to remain until I come, what *is that* to you?"

²⁴ This is the disciple who is bearing witness to these things and wrote these things, and we know that his witness is true.

²⁵ And there are also many other things which Jesus did, which if they *were written one after the other, I suppose that even the world itself *could not contain the books that *would be written.

50 Years of Translation History, Continued

LEGACY STANDARD BIBLE

"It is the best English translation I have ever read!"

- John MacArthur -

Discover more about the LSB, including the entire text online and a list of Bible apps that feature the translation at:

LSBible.org